On a Road

On a Road

A Poem Series
by Jim Landwehr

Copyright©2018 Jim Landwehr
All Rights Reserved

Published by Unsolicited Press
Portland, Oregon
www.unsolicitedpress.com

No part of this book may be reproduced or transmitted in any form or by any means without written permission from the publisher or author.

Printed in the United States of America.

Attention schools and businesses: for discounted copies on large orders, please contact the publisher directly.

ISBN: 978-1-947021-63-1

Contents

Foreword	1
Setting Pace	2
On A Road*	3
Sal's Paradise	4
Boys of Summer	5
Manhattan Beach	6
Crackin'	8
Hellywood	9
Rags to Riches	10
Of No Good Use to Anyone	11
St. Patrick's Day on the Edge of a Continent	12
Pacific Plastic	13
California Screamin'*	14
Lost Angeles	16
Breakfast in a Box	17
Sea and Sky	18
Mojave Exodus*	19
High in Colorado	20
Highballin' Missouri	21
Sucker Punch	22
Epilogue	23
Acknowledgements	25
About the Author	26

On a Road

Foreword

In March of 1984, two friends and I rented a car and drove nonstop from St. Paul, Minnesota to Los Angeles California, a forty-hour drive, one way. We were all in our early twenties and it was the first big trip for all of us. We worked together on the catalog dock at Montgomery Wards at the time and were visiting a former coworker who had relocated to the west coast.

The trip had elements of Jack Kerouac's classic novel, *On the Road*, and being a big fan of the beat generation, I decided to make a three-poem series out of my recollection of our travels. I chose to build in some references from Kerouac's work including changing my friends' names to match the characters in *On the Road*.

When I mentioned making the series into a larger work encompassing the entire trip, a colleague of mine encouraged me to follow through on it. It came together as a series of twenty vignettes that document the essence of the trip. The results are contained in this collection of work I have titled, *On a Road.*

Setting Pace

Sitting at the bar in southwest Minneapolis the boys and I realize we're starting the trip with recklessness and wonton disregard for schedule as we sip our beers, talk, and contemplate the estimated forty-hour trip we have in front of us.

Dean raises his glass and declares, "To California, boys!"

Sal and I echo back "To California!" and take long draws from our watered down American pilsners. We're just three twenty-somethings with highly uncertain futures doing what we do best at this point in our lives: drinking, hanging out, and living in the immediacy of the moment. If nothing else, we've got each other, these drinks and our collective dreams of palm trees, the Pacific Ocean, and So Cal girls on this grey day in March. I guess that will have to do for now. At the moment, everything is alright by me as the beer squelches the uncertainty of the road ahead and the jukebox plays Def Leppard's counsel to the lost boys of Minnesota.

We're here to burn out, not fade away.

On A Road*

Hurtling through the Nevada desert
three of us Midwest boys
in our twenties
haulin' ass in the middle of the night
in a rented '83 Chevy wagon four-banger.

We're jacked up on No Doz and Pepsi
thirty hours from the bar we started at
in Minnesota on our way to LA.

Erratic lights shimmer and dance
rocketing side to side, up and down
on the deserted horizon before us.

No one is sure what to think
but that sure ain't no plane.
It's a pleasant distraction from darkness
as we postulate and speculate:

An Area 51 experiment or legit UFO?
Maybe a No Doze overdose?

The Cavalier-on-loan screams ahead.
Golden Earring's Twilight Zone
thumps its bass beat onto
the factory-delivered stereo.
It's three AM and the night is long
as Sal, Dean, and I push toward LA.

Sal's Paradise

The Chevy rockets into the hills of
Albuquerque at night and we are
all bleary eyed and bucket-seat weary
but the beauty of the muted city lights
commands our full attention.
What a striking city, man!
Our drive-by assessment leads
Sal to profess that he would like
to live here
– and he's serious.
He is done with winter,
snow, cold, and nothingness.
The southwest terrain is so different
from what any of us has
ever seen.
None of us have ever been this far west.
It's all new, baby!
Yes, yes! Albuquerque is IT, he declares
as we throttle on through it
into the dry blackness.

Boys of Summer

In the parking lot of the local liquor store
the heat sears from the asphalt
near the dirty cavalier rental.
Sal is shirtless and clad in cutoff jeans
mixing ice and cheap vodka
with lemonade in a cooler
using the old eyeball method
creating a brain-crushing ratio
taste-tested on the fly
while Dean and I keep an eye out for cops.
We're headed to Manhattan Beach
to drink our lunch,
blast the ghetto box,
swim in the pacific surf, and
check out the bikinis of March
because Minnesota has no ocean, palm trees, or
bikinis worth a damn —
this is living.
I dig life! Dig it!

Manhattan Beach

It lay there in front of us
in aquamarine vastness.
The Pacific Ocean, man!
The reason we drove two thousand miles!
The edge of our country
with nothing but shades of blue;
cerulean, deep blue, and blue-green.
We lay in the sun like homeless derelicts,
drink sneaky pinks and
play some beach volleyball.
This lady friend of Damion's
says to me, *"You're German, right?"*
and keeps mentioning it
despite my repeated answers--
says my eyes give it away.
I think she's sweet on me,
but Damion warns
she's a flake, a real whack.

Later, Dean and I go body surfing-and people gawk.
The locals don't go in the water in winter.
Winter! They call this winter!
The whole ocean is ours
and we have taken to being
half vodka drunk
floundering in the sea.
Our bodies pummeled by
the pounding salty surf and it feels

like the fingers of heaven.
I could drown out here
and everything would be all right.

Crackin'

Sitting on Damion's patio deck crackin' some beers in the California sun because right now, life is good. It sure beats the snowcapped prairies of Minnesota we left back in our frozen homeland. Near as I can determine, this is heaven on earth, this place of palms, lizards, and orange trees in your neighbor's yard.

We ask Damion about the cracks in the concrete patio beneath our feet and he says,

"It's commonplace around here."

Quakes, baby!

This place is floating on a layer of magma just waiting for the big one. Maybe it ain't heaven after all.

Or maybe heaven comes with contingencies.

In any case, at this moment in '84,

So Cal is pretty damn close to it for these Midwest hicks.

Hellywood

We're on our way to see a bit of Hollywood
maybe find out what the big attraction is.
Sal's driving down some six-lane holocaust
through miles of Calighetto in our Chevy -
it just goes on and on:
the blight
rundown buildings
trash in the gutter
barred windows
last ditch cars with junkyard fenders
duct-taped plastic windows
boarded up buildings
razor wire
and gates on every door.
For godssake,
even the sorry looking palm trees
long for the suburbs to try and get out of
this shithole. California is its own kind of
gecko - changing colors without warning
and lying motionless in the hot sun.
It seems we've got to go through
hell to get to Hollywood.

Rags to Riches

This is where it's at, man!
Hollywood Boulevard. Dig it!
The walk of stars
Chinese Mann theatre
celebrity prints set in concrete
mansions of the stars and starlets
-*hey look, there's Elvis!*-
there's nothing like this back home
a freakshow of fame
mixed in with the normal LA madmen
and the drunken losers hidden in shadows.
Tour buses, T-shirts, and maps to the stars homes
everyone is looking to take your money
where millionaires live alongside
the shopping cart mobile homeless.
It's a land of have's, have mores,
and plenty of want mores.
Beneath everything cool and unusual
there is a cold reality
a heartbeat of hurt
hidden by the candy-coated
fast life of sex, drugs, and rock and roll.
This is my west coast enigma.

Of No Good Use to Anyone

In Damion's living room, Foghat blares
from his rocking stereo as I wait for
Sal to pass the pipe my way.
Damion scored some killer smoke – Tea! -
from an unnamed friend and is as
high as the rest of us – in fact,
he's in full-fledged paranoia mode
peeking out through the curtains.
Unlike us, he's got a real job
a true-to-life grownup job-
electrical engineer or some bullshit
for a government military weapon-building
corporate hell-hole and he's worried
someone's going to bust down the door
make him piss in a bottle
take away his job
and interrogate him to death.
Dean tells him to mellow out as I
choke a toke and mention that
my ears feel all rubbery.
Sal cracks up and says
"Dude…you are stoned, man!"
Dig it!

St. Patrick's Day on the Edge of a Continent

Sitting in an open air "fern bar"
drinking green beer
on Saint Patrick's Day
while MTV
blares those lip-synced abomination
music videos
from a multitude of TV's.
One minute
Peter Gabriel's *Shocking the Monkey*
and the next
Thomas Dolby is *Blinded by Science*
while we are killing west coast time
one of the only ways we
can think of – working on
tomorrow's hangover.
California's been hazy since
our arrival and I'm not
talking about the smog-
this whole trip reminds me
a constant rerun of the
drunk chapters of
A Sun Also Rises.
But I'm diggin' it
and can't wait to see where
it takes us next.

Pacific Plastic

The four of us fellas
had a nice Italian meal
at a place by the ocean,
and now we're at the dance club in
hopes of meeting some ladies.
Instead, it seems a lot like we're
paying too much for beers in trade
for a handful of LA rejections.
Girls seem cold in Cali-
in this land of superficiality,
money,
cars,
and hedonism
that oozes from the pores of people.
The whole deal is like cheap plastic.
If Minnesota's got nothing else,
the girls are warm and beautiful.
This California cool thing,
a faux paradise of celluloid dreams,
is wearing thin on me and the boys
and we're only three days in.

California Screamin'*

It is twelve lanes of southern California hell.
The traffic at one thirty in the morning
haulin' at twenty over the limit
makes rush hours back home look weak.
Sal fiddles with Damion's kickin' stereo
while Dean pushes the Trans Am hard
to keep up with the damned LA maniacs--
lane turtles buzz during inattentive drifts
keeping Dean-O honest and alert-
a cool reminder that he shouldn't be driving
but he is the best of the three of us
and that ain't sayin' much.
Damion, getting lucky back at the
San Fernando valley blowout we'd left,
surrendered the Pontiac keys to Dean-
said he'd find a way to get back home
tomorrow after his bimbo tango in the valley.
So here we are, three Minnesota hicks
screaming alongside Deloreans and screen stars
in a friend's horse powered rocket
somewhere between euphoric righteousness
and the Hollywood bowl.
"Put on some Van Halen," I scream
because that'll help and we're living
in someone else's toxic dream right now.
Sal fumbles with the cassette deck
and a half mile later we're in "Panama".
Yeah, we're runnin' the Trans Am hot tonight.

A regular hell is L.A.

Lost Angeles

Three of us woke up this morning to find ourselves
parked in Damion's Trans Am on a subdivision street
somewhere in our Lost Angeles
having arrived here after collectively
agreeing that, given Dean's condition, we had
no place on any road – especially the twelve-lane
fire breathing dragon that was freeway 405-
there's nothing freeing about it.
Last night's bohemian drunken drag out in the
San Fernando valley, with the psychedelic
brownies, the beautiful-but-snobbish chicks,
and too many beers to count, brought us here.
When we left, we were given the keys,
a small handful of half-assed directions, and
the two beers stuffed in Sal's shirt pocket
that might come in handy later.
Then wished good luck and sent into the
Southern California night
only to end up parked on a subdivision street
sleeping it off
somewhere in our Lost Angeles.

Breakfast in a Box

Somehow, we ended up at a Jack in the Box-
a dumpy hut-like fast food joint
which, frankly, none of us had heard of
prior to this alcohol-fogged trip to the coast.
But, they serve breakfast, so here we are.
The place isn't open yet
And we're loitering in the parking lot
in what would look quite convincingly
like a stolen Pontiac Trans Am
-no, really officer, it's our friend's car;
disregard those beers in Sal's pockets.
It might be a tough sell.
The three of us followed a road map
to get us back to Redondo Beach
after a little shuteye in a distant
suburb overnight.
What a night!
When the place finally opens
we order some chow to beat back our hangovers
while Dean finds a payphone and
makes a call to Damion back in the valley
-Hey, what's up man?
Yeah, your car's fine — we slept in it.
But somehow, we ended up at a Jack in the Box.

Sea and Sky

Standing on the deck of the Queen Mary-
The Queen! Diggin' her! -
she's in her full glory today
or as full as a dry-docked
steel-hulled behemoth can be.
She should be sailing
not parked like some aging broken down Caddy
with spoke wheel hubcaps.
Before this, we took a trip through
the Spruce Goose —
the Flying Boat! -
some Howard Hughes funded
proof-of-concept boondoggle
that only flew once, anyway.
The bird is glorious today too -
but more like a grounded albatross
waiting to stretch his wings
but unsure if he's up for the task.
Yes, yes!
These floating and flying
wonders of man deserve
California as much as
us Minnesota hicks
on a road
in the prime of our youth
chasing some celluloid dream
before we end up dry-docked
or grounded in our old age.

Mojave Exodus*

The '83 Chevy's paint is laden with dusty talc dirt from the road and the sin of our week as we speed out of the sand and sage. We are headed out of this godforsaken stretch of no-man's land known as the Mojave Desert into the bigger no-man's land of Las Vegas. My head thrums and sloshes a reminder of last night's knock-down, drag-out last hurrah beer binge at Damion's place back in LA.

What a night!

We saunter into the Barbary Coast casino to gamble and do a bit of involuntary second-hand smoking for a couple of hours before we head home. Low on cash and as broke as freelance poets on welfare, Sal and I plug quarter slots and slowly whittle away at our shares of the next tanks of gas. Meanwhile, Dean goes high rolling - dollar slots - picking the machine targeted at Minnesota tourists. On a string of bad luck he wires home for more money – twice.

When we are finished trading perfectly good hard-earned cash for a liberal dose of self-loathing and a mysterious spot on our left lung, we head back into the blast furnace, precipice of hell that this godforsaken place calls a climate. Standing there amidst all the depravity this city has to offer, I have to confess that a stop in Vegas sounded a whole lot better during the planning stages, half a country away.

High in Colorado

As luck would have it
we're passing through arguably the most beautiful
majestic part of our eighty-hour journey
in the middle of the night.
Colorado is passing underneath our wheels
but we can't see anything further than the
Chevy's weak headlights will reveal.
Our four-banger jalopy whines for mercy
as it struggles to climb these Rockies
at sixty miles an hour with a full load
and a week's worth of getting the piss beaten out of it;
treated like a rental.
At a wayside, Sal pulls over and
plugs an emergency spotlight into the lighter
and shines it on the sheer rock face.
Holy cats!
We stand there in the dark
gaping at the wonder of creation before us.
What a country we've seen on this road,
how much more a country we have not.

Highballin' Missouri

Outside Kansas City
barreling home at sixty-five
burning the rented cavalier
to the ground.
Burn it, baby!
Kansas City, here we come,
on our way back home
to the cold and the barren,
faceless plains of the Midwest.
Back to simple sanity
and living within a man's means.
Back to where people are as real
as God almighty intended –
no airs -
what you see is what you get.
Ten days on the road and
we've had about enough of
each other's company
as much as we can stand
and we're itching to get back
to our realities and sober lives
because while California is sweet
and dreamy and cool
it ain't home.

Sucker Punch

Rolling into our hometown
exhausted, road weary,
hungry, and nearly broke
looking for a car wash
and a place to fill the tank
of our rental car —
she's beat!
We get her washed up
looking like new
except for that mysterious ding
in the air dam up front.
None of us is sure who's to blame
and we're hoping that the rental rep
doesn't see it and ding *us!*
After checking the odometer
the poor sucker exclaims,
"Forty-five hundred miles in a week!
Where the hell did you go?"
Heh, just a little trip to LA-
contract said unlimited miles.
She might need an oil change-
Yes, yes!

Epilogue

Sitting at mom's house
thinking about the trip.
It almost seems surreal-
a Disneyland dream
but hazier like a smog fog
when you're drunk on LA beer
walking miles and miles of pavement.
Did it all really happen?
Or, maybe, what just happened?
It was a freakshow apparition
on the edge of the earth
and I'm wrestling with what it all means.
Meanwhile, Camille asks
if Dean and I could talk to Sal,
who it seems, is obsessed with
the thought of moving to LA;
I get it —
the place is hypnotic.
It draws and pulls from the east
with tectonic force.
The lures of palms and sun
money and fame,
but Dean and I know
it ain't us —
no way.
Home is home.
But this fantastic journey
with wild young madmen

in a cracker box car
pushes me to see
the endless possibilities
on a road out of town.

Acknowledgements

Pg. 3   *On a Road was previously published in *Reciting From Memory*

Pg. 14 *California Screamin' was previously published in *Reciting From Memory*

Pg. 19 *Mojave Exodus was previously published in *Reciting From Memory*

This entire work is in acknowledgement of, and with the utmost respect for, Jack Kerouac's classic book *On the Road*. It was in part compiled to pay tribute to the stylistic genius and ingenuity of that work and is in no way an attempt to diminish its importance in the history of American literature. I also owe a debt of gratitude to my traveling companions, Dean, Sal and Damion for creating the memories that fueled this work. And, finally, I thank the entire staff at Unsolicited Press for believing in my work and making this chapbook a reality.

About the Author

Jim has two nonfiction books, *Dirty Shirt: A Boundary Waters Memoir* and *The Portland House: A '70s Memoir*. Jim also has two poetry collections, *Reciting from Memory*, and *Written Life* as well as a chapbook, *On a Road*. His non-fiction stories have been published in *Main Street Rag*, *Prairie Rose Publications*, *Steam Ticket* and others. His poetry has been featured in *Torrid Literature Journal*, *Portage Magazine*, *Blue Heron Review* and many others. He lives in Waukesha, Wisconsin with his wife Donna and their two children. He enjoys fishing, kayaking, biking, and camping. Jim is poet laureate for the Village of Wales, Wisconsin.

www.ingramcontent.com/pod-product-compliance
Lightning Source LLC
Chambersburg PA
CBHW071759080526
44588CB00013B/2305